Door into the Sacred

Also by Paul Murray:

I Loved Jesus in the Night: Teresa of Calcutta, a Secret Revealed

Door into the Sacred

A Meditation on the Hail Mary

Paul Murray OP

DARTON·LONGMAN+TODD

First published in 2010 by
Darton, Longman and Todd Ltd
1 Spencer Court
140 – 142 Wandsworth High Street
London SW18 4JJ

© 2010 by Paul Murray

The right of Paul Murray to be identified as the Author
of this work has been asserted in accordance with the
Copyright, Designs and Patents Act 1998.

ISBN 978-0-232-52795-7

A catalogue record for this book is available from
the British Library

Extract from 'Annunciation' by Denise Levertov, from *A Door in the Hive*, copyright © 1989 by Denise Levertov. Reprinted by permission of New Directions Publishing Corps.

Typeset by Kerrypress Ltd, Luton, Bedfordshire
Printed and bound in Great Britain by Cromwell Press Group,
Trowbridge, Wiltshire

Detail of Heaven from the Last Judgement by Fra Angelico (Guido di Pietro) (*c*.1387-1455). Museo di San Marco dell'Angelico, Florence, Italy/The Bridgeman Art Library.

To my three sisters
Margaret, Isabel and Sally.
My three brothers
Billy, Myles and John.
And in memory of my brother
Jim.

Contents

Preface by Wojciech Giertych OP ... ix
Acknowledgments ... xii

Introduction ... 1

Part I: A Gospel Prayer ... 5

1 'Hail Mary, full of grace!' ... 9
2 'The Lord is with you!' ... 18
3 'Blessed are you among women!' ... 30
4 'Blessed is the fruit of your womb, Jesus!' ... 38

Part II: A Prayer of the People ... 45

5 'Holy Mary, Mother of God' ... 48
6 'Pray for us sinners' ... 58
7 'Now and at the hour of our death' ... 68

Notes ... 72

Preface

Perhaps the intuition that touched me most, as I read this booklet, was the author's happy insistence – following the insistence of St Bernadette Soubirous – on Mary's youthfulness at the moment of the Annunciation. There is something in youth that allows one easily to accept that which is freely given. As we grow older, we start to think in terms of merit, due, mutual obligations, faults and rights. But the young receive for nothing. They are spontaneously grateful for what they have received, living out playfully their filial response. It is this that Fr Paul Murray OP notes in Mary's encounter with God, as the angel speaks out the first word of God in the new dispensation: 'Rejoice, you who have been gifted!' Everything else, questioning, intellectual reflection, the return gifts or faithful perseverance even in suffering come later, after that initial, trustful and joyful belief that one has been freely graced. St Paul's switch from viewing life in the perspective of the Law of Moses, to the viewing of life in the perspective of the alliance made by God with Abraham at a time when the Law had not yet been given belongs to that same spiritual joy of the freely graced.

This initial spiritual experience of Mary is recognised as fundamental in one of the most popular of Christian prayers, the Ave Maria. It finds an echo not only in human hearts, in the simplest of Christian devotions, but also in sublime Christian art and music. We, who are Mary's children, not conceived physically beneath her heart, but adopted, and therefore located within, not under her heart, are invited by her, and by the Church, and by this book too, to persevere in that youthful, spontaneous and un-travailed gratitude for the simple fact that God's graces precede us, lead us, are working in us and accompany us, both in the continuously repeated now and in the future hour of our death.

Wojciech Giertych OP
Theologian of the Papal Household

Detail of Heaven from the Last Judgement by Fra Angelico (Guido di Pietro) (c.1387-1455). Museo di San Marco dell'Angelico, Florence, Italy/The Bridgeman Art Library.

Acknowledgments

My thanks goes first of all to Fr. Wojciech Giertych, OP, the theologian of the Papal Household, for kindly agreeing to write a Preface to this tiny book. I am also grateful to the following friends and colleagues for their encouragement and support: Breda Ennis, Sr Katherine Elena Wolff, Ron and Concetta Solomine, Jim and Jennifer Klatt, Patrick Pye, Philip McShane, OP and Arnfin Haram, OP.

St Thomas Aquinas tells us that there should be no limit to expressing our gratitude to those men and women from whom we have received favours of one kind or another. I am happy, therefore, to seize this opportunity to thank my three Dominican Sisters, Edith, Helen, and Josephine, of the Holy Rosary Province (Phillipines) for the example of prayer they give to myself and to all the priests living at the Convitto of St Thomas in Rome. I would also like to thank, for their prayerful encouragement and practical assistance, Fr Luke Buckles OP, and Shine Raju.

Introduction

For almost an entire millennium the most commonly repeated prayer in the Church, apart from the Our Father, has been the Hail Mary. It's a prayer that, with great simplicity and ease, brings us at once into the mystery of God incarnate, the mystery of Jesus, son of Mary. But if we compare this prayer with the great and sacred prayers of the liturgy, the Hail Mary appears as a very tiny door indeed, a humble entrance. But it is, all the same, an entrance. Though small it has, again and again, and for countless numbers of people over the centuries, proved to be a privileged threshold of grace, a real opening into the mystery and meaning of God's love, a 'holy door'.

The Hail Mary is a prayer which is easy to say, easy to pray. It contains and expresses a profound and simple heartfelt devotion. But it also contains, as I hope to demonstrate in these pages, a radiance and depth of theological truth which are no less integral to its character. One clear indication of this fact is that even as outstanding a theologian as St Thomas Aquinas chose, at one point in his life, to dedicate time to a thoughtful and illuminating reflection on the Ave Maria.[1] In more recent centuries, however, theologians have been a lot less inclined to give attention to the humbler forms and practices of Christian devotion. Their theology has tended, as a result, to become rather dry and abstract, their writing so insistently dull, at times, and uninspiring, as to be almost unrelated to a path of spirituality, their thoughts and theories out of contact with living faith experience.

At the same time, and not perhaps surprisingly, the life of devotion itself has suffered from this separation. Deprived of contact with the sanity and challenge of a robust intellectual tradition, many of the more popular devotional practices within the Church have tended to assume exaggerated and sentimental forms. No wonder, then, that one of the most celebrated theologians of the twentieth century, Hans Urs von Balthasar, could go so far as to declare, in the summer of 1984: 'I insist on the inseparability between theology and spirituality, their separation being the worst disaster that ever occurred in the history of the Church.'[2]

My hope in writing this tiny book is that, by giving space to some of the most moving and most profound reflections ever written on the Hail Mary, a door will open for the reader into a world in which the strenuous task of thinking and the easeful grace of feeling can both be considered sacred, and where wisdom and enchantment, theology and devotion, are found, at core, to be one and the same thing.

Part I

A Gospel Prayer

Hail Mary,
Full of grace, the Lord is with you.
Blessed are you among women
and blessed is the fruit of your womb,
Jesus.

We are accustomed to thinking of these two short sentences as forming merely the first part of the 'Hail Mary'. But, in fact, these few words constituted the entire prayer right up to the end of the fourteenth century. The prayer, as we know it today, with the added prayer of petition, 'Holy Mary, Mother of God, pray for us sinners' etc., did not take final shape until the end of the fifteenth century. In its earlier, shorter form the prayer possesses a manifestly simple and direct Gospel character. It consists of two greetings — two joyful salutations — addressed to Mary, both taken from the Gospel of Luke (1:28 and 1:42). Exactly when these two Lucan sentences were brought together for the first time to form the brief prayer, known later as the Ave Maria, is impossible to determine. But what is clear is that, already by the sixth century, the two greetings were united in a single prayer-formula, and introduced into a number of the liturgies of the East. Meanwhile, in the West, this tiny Gospel invocation makes an appearance as an Offertory antiphon for the Feast of the Annunciation and for the Fourth Sunday of Advent. As time passed, the prayer began to be recited in a new way, no longer simply as a brief meditation in the public liturgy but also in private, as a form of personal devotion, and by different kinds of people, both monastic and lay. The name 'Jesus' was added to the prayer, it is believed, in or around the year 1263.[3]

****

For all its simplicity this first part of the Hail Mary is really a rather unusual prayer: *Hail Mary, full of grace, the Lord is with you. Blessed are you among women, and blessed is the fruit of your womb.* Strictly speaking, this is not a prayer of petition or a prayer of praise; it is not even a prayer of thanksgiving or a confession of faith. At root, it is simply a greeting: 'Hail Mary!' What the prayer encourages us to say is, first and last, a simple 'hello'. 'Hail Mary, full of grace, the Lord is with you!' It suggests a meeting of real joy, a way of saying to someone we love, saying to Mary in this case, 'What a delight, what a great pleasure it is to meet you!'

When it occurs, the word 'grace' – in the phrase 'full of grace' – carries with it not only the profound theological meaning of gift or favour, but also the idea of someone who possesses great beauty and great charm: 'Hail Mary, full of grace, the Lord is with you!' The deepest compliment we can give to someone we know, someone we love, is to say, 'The Lord is with you', which is another way of saying, 'When I meet you I am always somehow graced. I am a better person for having come to know you. In fact, I cannot ever meet you without, in some sense, meeting God.'

The words of salutation in this first part of the Hail Mary are taken, for the most part, directly from Scripture. The first greeting, for example, 'Hail Mary, full of grace, the Lord is with you', quite clearly echoes, although not in every detail, the salutation addressed to Mary by the angel Gabriel.[4] The second greeting, 'Blessed are you among women and blessed is the fruit of your womb', contains the actual words Elizabeth, in her joy, spoke to Mary the moment she saw her young cousin coming to meet her. So, as we begin our reflection, let us take these two Gospel statements and attend with as much care as we can to the meaning of each and every phrase. Later, we will turn our attention to the second part of the prayer, that part which emerged in later centuries out of the Church's living faith tradition.

Chapter 1

'Hail Mary, full of grace!'

By now we are so familiar with these words, and with the image of the angel Gabriel greeting Mary with reverence, that we almost take the scene for granted. But St Thomas Aquinas, in a homily devoted exclusively to the Ave Maria, remarked that, until the moment when the angel Gabriel greeted Mary in this way, 'it was unheard of that an angel should show reverence for a human being'.[5] Why, then, the unique respect for Mary? St Thomas explains that when the Angel 'paid reverence to Mary by saying *full of grace*', he was in effect saying, 'I bow to you because you surpass me in fullness of grace.'[6]

This encounter between Mary and the angel, evoked here by Aquinas, has been the subject of many paintings and poems since the early Middle Ages. In fact, one can say that this scene in the Gospel caught the imagination of Europe like almost no other. Consider, for example, the following words of wonder and amazement which we find on the lips of the archangel Gabriel in the famous Akathistos Hymn of the sixth century. 'A leading angel', we're told, 'was sent from heaven to say to the Virgin "Hail". And when he came he was amazed and arose and cried to her with voice incorporeal':

Hail to you through whom joy will shine out;
hail to you through whom the curse will pass away;
hail, redemption of fallen Adam;
hail, deliverance of the tears of Eve;
hail, height unattainable by human thought;
hail, depth invisible even to the eyes of angels;
hail to you, the throne of the king;
hail to you who bear him the bearer of all;
hail, star that heralds the sun;
hail, womb of divine incarnation;
hail to you through whom creation is reborn;
hail to you through whom the Creator becomes a child.[7]

In this remarkable incantation, Mary is honoured not only as a wondrous sign of the Incarnation but also as a unique participant within the mystery. She not only bears witness to the Son of God, she actually bears him in her flesh, and that is what prompts, of course, the ecstatic litany in her honour. In contrast, the first

'HAIL MARY, FULL OF GRACE!'

words of the Hail Mary state simply, 'Hail Mary, full of grace!' Mary has many wonderful titles given to her by the Church and by tradition, but when we begin this prayer we address her simply and directly by her first name, 'Mary': 'Hail Mary, full of grace!' Mary is, of course, 'the first among the redeemed', and the greatest of our race. But, although she has received a glory almost impossible to express, Mary remains, even now, recognisably herself, a woman, a mother, a human being. Yes, she has been raised up by God, and is now radiant in the glory of heaven, but her heart though changed is still the same. Mary never loses contact, not even for a moment, with the young woman she was in Nazareth at the time of the Annunciation.

Julian of Norwich, the celebrated English mystic of the Middle Ages, reflecting on this mystery, and also on a vision she received concerning Mary, writes:

> [O]ur Lord God ... showed me Our Lady, St Mary, and the true and outstanding wisdom which made her gaze on her Maker, so great, high, mighty, and good. The greatness and splendour of her vision of God filled her with holy dread, and caused her to see herself for the insignificant, lowly, simple creature she was compared with her

Lord God. And holy dread filled her with humility. Because of this basic humility she was filled with grace and every virtue, thereby surpassing all creation.[8]

And again:

> God brought Our Lady to my understanding. I saw her [as] ... a simple, humble girl, young in years, of the stature which she had when she conceived.

And:

> [Mary] beheld her God, marvelling with great reverence that he was willing to be born of her who was a simple creature created by him.[9]

A point worth noting here in passing is that the form in which Mary, the Mother of God, appeared to Bernadette Soubirous of Lourdes in 1858 was not that of a mature and stately lady (as people at the time wanted to believe), but rather that of a very young and exceptionally beautiful girl.[10] The stone statue we see today in the niche at the Grotto at Lourdes was, as it happens, much criticised by Bernadette. One of her objections was that 'the girl' of the visions had somehow been transformed into a much older-looking figure. And into a *colder* figure. *Young* was how she characterised the radiant girl she saw at Massabielle, and that's exactly how she reported the vision when she first met with the sculptor of the statue, Joseph Fabish.[11] Unfortunately, however, it appears Fabish took little or no account of this testimony, believing, like most of his contemporaries, that the Virgin must surely have appeared to Bernadette as a 'grown-up'. But so young, in fact, and so small in stature, was the bright, mysterious figure in the rock at Massabielle, Bernadette chose later to describe her as 'pétito damizélo' (a petite young maiden).[12] It is, therefore, no exaggeration to say that, in her apparition at Lourdes, Mary assumed something of the actual form and stature she possessed as a young girl when she first conceived.

That thought I find to be as telling and as beautiful as it is unexpected. But the idea is, of course, one that corresponds exactly with the experience of Julian of Norwich five centuries earlier. The shining figure that appeared to Bernadette was not that of the solemn 'Lady' of popular imagination but rather that of the young Mary, the young 'virgin' of Luke's gospel. No wonder, then, that when, on 25 March 1858, the Feast of the Annunciation, Mary appeared to Bernadette, she was able to reveal her identity with such simple candour and authority, speaking not only with her words but with her very form: *Que soy era Immaculada Conceptciou.* 'I am the Immaculate Conception.'[13]

****

One of the things I never like to contemplate for too long, when preaching at Mass, or preaching anywhere, is just what the saints of God in the congregation are making of my attempt to communicate the Gospel. Think of the possibility, for example, that while you, as preacher, are delivering your homily, down beneath you a tiny figure, someone say like the great Thérèse of Lisieux, or the young Bernadette Soubirous, is there in among the congregation, and is quietly gazing up at you! I make this observation here because, with regard to Mary, Thérèse, as it happens, had very strong views indeed on just what the preacher *should* be talking about. To one of her sisters, in fact, talking about some of the fanciful and florid sermons on Mary that she had heard given by priests over the years, but that had clearly left her cold, she remarked: 'We have had enough of that sort of thing: "*on en a assez!*" '[14]

> How much I would have liked to be a priest so that I might have preached about the Blessed Virgin! One occasion would have

been sufficient to say all that I think on that subject. I would show, first of all, how little the life of the Blessed Virgin is known. We should refrain from saying improbable things about her or things we know nothing about ... If a sermon on the Blessed Virgin is to appeal to me, and to bear fruit, I need to see the life she actually lived [as indicated in the Gospel] and not as fabricated by imagination.[15]

The exasperation of Thérèse, finding herself compelled to listen to the fictions and fancies propagated by the preachers of her time, is a form of frustration not unlike that experienced, centuries earlier, by St Thomas Aquinas. Asked, on one occasion, by a fellow Dominican preacher, if it was true that Mary, during her life, had repeated with enormous sorrow the words 'a sword shall pierce your own soul' seven times a day, Thomas replied — and with more than a hint of impatience — that the suggestion had no known authority behind it. 'In my opinion,' he declared, 'such frivolities ought not to be preached, seeing there are so many subjects for preaching that are absolutely true.'[16] Thérèse, the 'little' Doctor, was clearly of one mind with Aquinas on this point. She remarked: '[Mary] lived a life of faith common to all of us, and this should be made clear from what we read in the Gospel.' And again: 'I am certain that the life she actually lived was quite ordinary ... She is pictured as if she were unapproachable, but she needs to be shown as someone whom it is possible to imitate by practising her hidden virtues.'[17]

Pope Paul VI, in his Apostolic Exhortation *Marialis Cultus*, also spoke of the 'solid evangelical virtues' of Mary, her 'faith' and 'generous obedience', her 'genuine humility', her 'fortitude in exile and suffering', her 'poverty and trust in God', her 'solicitous charity', her 'delicate forethought', and her 'profound wisdom'.[18] Obviously, in all of these things, Mary is our practical example and inspiration. But she is also, needless to say, beyond us in so many other ways. When, in the Ave Maria, we who are the disciples of Jesus call her simply 'Mary', we are reminded of God's care for the lowly, and that even the least of the disciples among us can hope to be raised up by God's mercy, and have some share in the fullness of grace. Ildephonsus of Toledo, a seventh-century monk, conscious of the healing grace which he himself had received from the incarnate Son of God, turns to Mary the mother of his Lord, in wonder and gratitude, and exclaims: 'To become my Redeemer, he became your Son. To become the price of my redemption, his Incarnation took place from your flesh. From your flesh he took a body that would be wounded that he might heal my wounds.'[19] And, later, in the same text, referring to himself as 'a lowly man,' he writes:

> I pray you, O holy Virgin, that I might possess Jesus from that same Spirit by which you gave birth to Jesus. Through that Spirit, through which your flesh conceived Jesus, may my soul accept Jesus. By that Spirit by which you were able to know and give birth to Jesus, may I be granted to know Jesus… You professed yourself to be the handmaid of the Lord, desiring that it be done to you according to the angel's word; in that same Spirit, may I, a lowly man, speak lofty things of Jesus.[20]

Chapter 2

'The Lord is with You!'

These words, and the meaning of these words, have been so wonderfully illustrated by painters over the centuries that, when we try to meditate on the meeting between Mary and the angel, it is inevitable that we will have before our eyes the memory of some beautifully painted image or radiant icon. But the scene at the Annunciation has also been 'painted' for us in sound as well as in colour, in words as well as in images. The Akathistos Hymn, which I quoted earlier, is the most famous prayer or poem of this kind. But already, as early as the fourth century, we find in one of the homilies of St Gregory of Nyssa, for example, a passage in which Gregory encourages the people not simply to look at the Annunciation scene from outside, but rather to enter into the mystery directly, as it were, and to repeat together as a community the words addressed to Mary. Thus, at a key point in his homily, St Gregory exclaims:

> At the top of our voice let us say, along with the angel, Rejoice, full of grace, the Lord is with you ... with the servant, the king; with the immaculate, the one who sanctifies the whole world; with the beautiful, the most beautiful among the sons of men!.[21]

A short, meditative poem composed by the twentieth-century Catholic author Denise Levertov paints for us a no less vivid picture of the scene at the Annunciation. Here's how the poem begins:

We know the scene: the room, variously furnished,
almost always a lectern, a book; always
the tall lily.
    Arrived on solemn grandeur of great wings,
the angelic ambassador, standing or hovering,
whom she acknowledges, a guest.

But we are told of meek obedience. No one mentions courage.
    The engendering Spirit
did not enter her without consent.
                    God waited.[22]

Later in the poem, Levertov writes: 'This was the minute no one speaks of, / when she could still refuse.'[23] But Mary accepted 'the astounding ministry she was offered':[24]

> ... to carry
> in hidden, finite inwardness,
> nine months of Eternity ...
>   Then bring to birth,
> push out into air, a Man-child
> needing, like any other,
> milk and love —
> but who was God.[25]

Levertov's earlier statement, 'God waited', brings to mind at once certain lines from a famous homily by St Bernard of Clairvaux on the Annunciation. Addressing Mary directly, Bernard exclaims:

> You have heard that you shall conceive and bear a Son; you have heard that you shall conceive, not of man, but of the Holy Spirit. The angel is waiting for your answer: it is time for him to return to the God who sent him. We, too, are waiting, O Lady, for the word of pity, even we who are overwhelmed in wretchedness ... by one little word of yours in answer shall we all be made alive ... Answer, O Virgin, answer the

angel speedily; rather, through the angel, answer your Lord. Speak the word, and receive the Word; offer what is yours, and conceive what is of God; give what is temporal, and embrace what is eternal.[26]

What was being asked of Mary was something extraordinary. But Levertov, the poet, reminds us that sooner or later all of us are confronted by a demand we would rather avoid:

> Aren't there annunciations
>   of one sort or another
>   in most lives?
>   Some unwillingly
>   undertake great destinies,
>   enact them in sullen pride,
>   uncomprehending.
>   More often
>   those moments
>   when roads of light and storm
>   open from darkness in a man or woman,
> are turned away from
> in dread, in a wave of weakness, in despair
> and with relief.[27]

According to Levertov, when we come face to face with the challenge of our own 'annunciation', very often we turn away, unable to come to terms with what is being asked of us. 'Ordinary lives continue,' Levertov writes, 'But the gates close, the pathway vanishes.'[28] In contrast, Mary's response at the Annunciation was marked by a great courage: 'Called to a destiny more momentous / than any in all of Time, / She did not quail.'[29]

> She did not cry, 'I cannot, I am not worthy',
> nor, 'I have not the strength' …
> Bravest of all humans,
>   consent illumined her.
> The room was filled with its light,
> the lily glowed in it,
>   and the iridescent wings.
> Consent,
>   courage unparalled,
> opened her utterly.[30]

Before she surrendered her will to God at the Annunciation, Mary first put a question to the angel: 'How can this be?' She was not, of course, demanding a full rational explanation before she gave her momentous fiat and said 'Yes'. Reflecting on this act of surrender on the part of Mary at the Annunciation, St Teresa of Avila writes:

'THE LORD IS WITH YOU!'

> [Mary] did not act as do some learned men ... for they want to be so rational about things and so precise in their understanding that it doesn't seem anyone else but they with their learning can understand the grandeurs of God. If only they would learn the humility of the most Blessed Virgin![31]

So Mary put her whole trust in the Word that came to her from heaven, and surrendered. This act of surrender is something we find particularly hard to do. All the more striking, therefore, is the following brief observation made by Meister Eckhart, one of the most famous Catholic mystics and intellectuals of the Middle Ages. He writes: 'One Hail Mary said when a man has abandoned himself is more profitable than to read the Psalms a thousand times over.'[32]

Illuminating also in this context is the account of a visit made to Calcutta by an American priest several years ago. In part, his visit was undertaken with the hope of meeting Mother Teresa. But he also had a big decision to make. So, in a sense, it was his moment of 'annunciation'. The first thing he did in Calcutta was to make a long retreat. And, then, when it was over, he went to see Mother Teresa. He asked her to pray for him. 'What do you want me to pray for?' she asked. 'For clarity of mind,' he replied. 'No, I won't!' she answered — a reply which must have completely astonished him. 'I will pray', she said, 'that you will have trust.'

Of course, there is a time and a place also for using our minds, and for confronting head on some of the problems associated with our faith. Cardinal Newman, reflecting on the Annunciation of Mary, puts it very well when he says: 'Mary is our pattern of Faith, both in the reception and in the study of Divine Truth.'[33] And why? Because Mary 'pondered' the angel's message. Newman writes: 'She [Mary] does not think it enough to accept [the message], she dwells upon it ... not enough to assent, she develops it ... first believing without reasoning, next from love and reverence, reasoning after believing.'[34] Theology is vital, but it comes second. What is of the first and most fundamental importance for both Newman and Mother Teresa is a simple childlike trust. Newman calls it 'believing without reasoning'.

In this process whereby Mary is drawn first of all to surrender herself to God, and then later to start pondering the mystery, she is, we can say, being in some sense *evangelised* by the angel. On this point Ildephonsus of Toledo writes:

> You were visited by the angel, hailed by the angel, called blessed by the angel, troubled

by his words, absorbed in reflection, astonished by his greeting, and you marvelled at the words he spoke. You hear that you have found favour with God, and you are commanded not to be afraid; you are strengthened with confidence, instructed in knowledge of miracles, promoted to a new state of glory, hitherto unknown... What is to be born of you is holy and will be called Son of God — so the angel evangelizes you — and in a wonderful way you learn how great will be the power of the King to be born. You ask, 'How will this happen?' You enquire about the cause. You seek an explanation. You seek to know by experience. You enquire about how it will be arranged. Then hear his unheard-of oracle, consider the unusual work, note the unknown secret, attend to the unseen deed. The Holy Spirit will come upon you, and the power of the Most High will overshadow you (Lk 1:35). Invisibly, the entire Trinity will accomplish the conception within you. Only the Person of the Son of God is to be born in your body, and he alone will take flesh from you. And so what will be conceived in you, what will be born from you, what will come forth from you, what will be brought forth and delivered from you is holy and will be called Son of God. For he will be great; he will be the God of power; he the King of all the ages; he the Maker of all things.[35]

****

When we read the Gospel account of the Annunciation we discover that, according to the original Greek, the first word spoken by the Angel was not the word 'Hail', as in 'Hail Mary', but rather the word 'Chaire' which means 'Rejoice!'[36] This was one heavenly command or invitation, however, which Mary, at least at first, was unable to obey. The Gospel tells us, in fact, that far from experiencing within herself a great and immediate joy, Mary was 'deeply troubled'. She was bewildered – and understandably – a state of soul that would, from then on, be part and parcel of her life of faith. Of course, Mary knew enormous joy at times, but she also knew very great and terrible sorrow, even perhaps suffering a kind of depression after the torture and death of her Son. I don't make this suggestion here on my own authority, but on something I have read in the writings of St Teresa of Avila.

Once, when by her own admission Teresa was feeling particularly lonely and even somewhat depressed (it was Eastertime, and everyone else was rejoicing), she experienced God coming to console her after Holy Communion. And what he said to her gave her a remarkable insight into the bewilderment experienced by the mother of Jesus after the resurrection. Teresa writes:

> It seemed most clear that our Lord sat beside me and He began to console me with great favours, and He told me among other things: 'See Me here, daughter, for it is I; give me your hands.' And it seemed He took them and placed them on His side and said: 'Behold My wounds. You are not without Me.'[37]

Teresa then adds:

> He [Jesus] told me that immediately after His resurrection He went to see Our Lady because she then had great need and that the pain she experienced [earlier at His passion] so absorbed and trans-pierced her soul that she did not return immediately to rejoice in that joy... He also said that He had remained a long time with her because it was necessary in order to console her.[38]

What, in effect, Jesus was saying to Mary, his mother, was the same thing he said to Teresa in her loneliness and depression, and the same thing he wants to say to all of us, no matter how abandoned or how broken we may feel: 'You are not without me' – or, in other words, 'The Lord is with you.'

****

An Irish poet of the mid-eighth century ends a long, devotional meditation in praise of Jesus, the son of Mary, by speaking of the unspeakable suffering which she endured because of the passion and death of her only child. At one point, addressing directly the Mother of Jesus, the poet exclaims, 'I call you with honest words, Mary'. And, after naming her son as 'Christ the bright', he reveals the force and depth of his desire that Mary be consoled in her grief or, at least, in some way joined in her grief by others like himself:

> If I ruled with every honour
> earth's peoples to the far sea
> they would come with me and with you
> to lament your Son, the King.
>
> Men, women, children,

beating their hands without cease
in lament on the hills
for the King Who created the stars.

But I cannot: so I will mourn
your Son profoundly with you
if, at some time,
you will come to visit me.

That we may talk together
in the pity of an unstained heart,
O head of purest faith,
come to me, loving Mary.[39]

Chapter 3

'Blessed are you among women!'

When Mary was greeted in this way by her elderly cousin Elizabeth, she at once sang her Magnificat, that great song of joy and of self-knowledge in God: 'My soul glorifies the Lord, my spirit rejoices in the Lord God, my Saviour!' Mary was not able to respond in this way when she was greeted by the angel Gabriel. No – what in the end occasioned her joy were words spoken to her by Elizabeth, her elderly relative, very simple and very humble words of delighted recognition: 'Blessed are you among women, and blessed is the fruit of your womb!' There is here, if I'm not mistaken, an important but unexpected lesson. Sometimes we might be inclined to think that, without the confirmation of some interior vision or some deep experience in prayer, we cannot hope to know the joy of God's love for us. But Mary's experience at the Visitation reminds us that such a deep and joyful realisation can be the result of a simple good deed or act of generosity done to someone in need. Again and again, to our astonishment, we discover that it is in the poor, in those who need our help, that the Lord is waiting to fill us with the knowledge, the joyful knowledge, that we are loved.

And this knowledge is knowledge that heals. If we, who know ourselves to be wounded in some way, make an effort to help others who are suffering, if we 'share our bread with the hungry' and try to 'shelter the homeless poor' or make a visit to someone in need like Mary, then, according to the prophet Isaiah, not only will we experience enlightenment of some kind, but '[our] wound will quickly be healed over' (Isa. 58:6–8). And why? Because in those who are most in need of help we will meet Christ himself: 'Whatever you do to one of these, the least of my brothers, you do to me.' I remember, on one occasion, Mother Teresa taking my hand and, with her forefinger, spelling out this message on my fingers. 'The entire mystery', she said, 'is here, Fr Paul, in this one sentence: "You – did – it – to – me".' Then, she took my hand a second time, and repeated the exercise, this time with an even greater emphasis: 'You – did – it – to – me.' *Twice* – I think she must have realised I was a slow learner!

On another occasion Mother Teresa told me that, during her first weeks working with the poor in

Calcutta, something unusual happened. One night she had a very remarkable dream. Still to this day I can see the playful gleam in her eye as she was telling me the story. She found herself just outside the gates of heaven. Needless to say she was absolutely delighted. She thought the bliss of heaven was hers at last. But, suddenly, St Peter came out and stopped her at the gate. 'No, you can't come in here,' he said. 'There are no slums up here!' 'I was really angry with Peter', she told me. But then, in the next instant, she turned to Peter and said: 'All right, Peter, I will go back. But be sure of this: I will return here before long, and fill this heaven of yours with all of my people from the slums!'

****

When Mary sings her Magnificat she identifies, first and last, with the poorest of the poor, singing of a God of great power and compassion 'who casts down the mighty from their thrones and lifts up the lowly', who 'fills the starving with good things but sends the rich away empty'. This concern of Mary for the needy of this world, and for the most forgotten, is one which will be shared by all those who find themselves inspired by her example and by the words of her Magnificat to walk the same Gospel path, and to breathe the same Gospel spirit. Merely, therefore, to attempt to give her honour while, at the same time, choosing to ignore completely the problems of poverty and injustice in our world today is, in effect, to turn our backs on the poor, and to close our eyes and ears to the hunger and thirst of those with whom Christ, the Son of Mary, has most clearly identified.

An unusually strong and vivid text on devotion to Mary, composed in the seventeenth century, is worth referring to at this point. The work, which bears the challenging title, *Wholesome Advice from the Blessed Virgin to her Indiscreet Devotees*, is concerned with naming and criticising the excesses to which an exaggerated, over-sentimental piety will inevitably lead. The author, Adam Widenfeld, allows Mary, the Mother of God, to speak to us in the text *directly* as it were. And so, at one point in the work, we hear her saying: 'Do not think that the love one has for me is praiseworthy when my images are decked with stones and precious ornaments while Jesus Christ suffers in his poor, if he dies of hunger, of cold, in his members.'[40]

This extraordinary tract provoked enormous controversy in its day, openly attacking, as it did, what the author called 'the dry little devotions' and 'the easy and convenient piety' of some of the characteristic devotees of the Virgin Mary. Unfortunately, the tone of the tract, being so insistently negative throughout, gave the impression of being opposed to almost all forms of Marian devotion. That said, however, the particular passage voiced for Mary, which I have quoted above, is without question instinct with the wisdom and challenge of the Christian Gospel. A no less passionate concern for the forgotten poor distinguishes a homily delivered, centuries earlier, by the great saint and preacher John Chrysostom. The saint declared:

> Of what use is it to weigh down Christ's table with golden cups, when he himself is dying of hunger? First, fill him when he is hungry; then use the means you have left to adorn his table. Will you have a golden cup made but not give a cup of water? ... Do not, therefore, adorn the church and ignore your afflicted brother, for he is the most precious temple of all.[41]

****

In the New Testament there are certain people who are described as 'blessed': those, for example, to whom, on the last day, Jesus will say, 'Come, blessed of my Father, take for your heritage the kingdom prepared for you ... For I was hungry and you gave me food, thirsty and you gave me drink, a stranger and you made me welcome; naked and you clothed me, sick and you visited me, in prison and you came to see me.' These men and women are all clearly 'blessed'. But what is the difference between their experience of being blessed and that of Mary? When, in the Hail Mary, we recite the phrase, 'Blessed are you among women', seeking to identify ourselves with the great statement of Elizabeth, we are clearly acknowledging that Mary is someone uniquely favoured by God, uniquely blessed. 'Yes,' exclaims Gregory of Nyssa, 'you are indeed blessed among women: blessed because, among all other virgins, you have been chosen, and have been judged worthy to welcome such a Lord, and have received into yourself the One who fills all things.'[42] Writing about a century later, the Syrian poet-theologian Jacob of Serugh (*c.* 451–521) takes up this theme in his 'Hymn to the Virgin Mary':

> Blessed is she: she has become the temple where dwells the Son of the highest heavens
> ...
> Blessed is she: the limits of her womb have contained grandeur without limit ...
> Blessed is she: she has made a home in her womb for the One who stirs up the waves of the ocean.

> Blessed is she: she has carried that giant force which carries the world and embraced him, and covered him with tender caresses …
>
> Blessed is she: her lips have touched the One whose flame and radiance make even the burning Seraphim recoil.
>
> Blessed is she: she has been able to nourish with milk from her own breast the One who has given life to all the worlds.[43]

Mary's uniqueness, astonishing though it is, is not intended by God to diminish, even for a moment, the presence of his grace in the lives of others. On this point Thérèse of Lisieux declares:

> There is no need to say that, by virtue of her prerogatives, the Blessed Virgin will eclipse the glory of all the saints, as the sun, on its rising, makes the stars disappear. *Mon Dieu!* What a strange idea! A mother who makes her children's glory disappear! I think exactly the opposite – I think that she will very much increase the glory of the elect.[44]

By both nature and grace Mary is unique. She is without compare. But the quite extraordinary blessing which she has received from God does not obscure for a moment all the varieties of blessing which exist within the community of believers. On the contrary. If anything, her exaltation heightens our awareness of that manifold blessing. 'Do you want to see her,' the Lord asked Julian of Norwich on one occasion. And when he showed Mary to Julian, in that instant Julian realised something of supreme importance. God, as he was showing her 'the most desirable sight' in all creation, was saying to her, and saying to all of us: 'Can you see in her [in Mary] how greatly you are loved? For love of you I made her so exalted, so noble, so worthy.'[45] This remarkable thought finds expression also in one of the prayers addressed to Mary by the eleventh-century monk St Anselm. Quickened to wonder at the thought of the privilege of Mary but also at the thought of her astonishing bond with each one of us, he exclaims:

> You are blessed and exalted
> not for yourself alone but for us too.
> What great and loving thing is this
> that I see coming to us through you?[46]

Chapter 4

'Blessed is the fruit of your womb, Jesus!'

At this stage in our meditation, although we are still addressing Mary, the name 'Jesus' is spoken. We have come to the very heart of the prayer, to the hinge on which it turns. For the Hail Mary is nothing if not a doorway into the mystery of Christ. On this point, Pope John Paul II writes: 'The centre of gravity in the Hail Mary, the hinge as it were which joins its two parts, is *the name of Jesus*.'[47] And that name is, of course, as John Paul II goes on to state, 'the only name given to us by which we may hope for salvation'.[48] He writes: 'One thing is clear: although the repeated *Hail Mary* is addressed directly to Mary, it is to Jesus that the act of love is ultimately directed, with her and through her.'[49] In almost all the great Marian prayers, composed over the centuries, this point is made explicit. Thus, in the following lines from an ancient Irish poem attributed to St Columcille ('Invocation of the Blessed Virgin Mary'), although Mary is invoked as a 'door' and as a 'safeguard to the kingdom', the grace of the opening of that door is understood to depend, first and last, on the birth, death and resurrection of her Son, Christ Jesus.

> Choice door through which was born in
> flesh the shining sun
> whom all would choose, Jesus
> Son of the living God.
>
> For the sake of the beauteous One
> who was conceived in your womb
> for the sake of the Only-begotten
> who is High-King everywhere,
>
> For the sake of his cross, nobler
> than all crosses, for the sake of
> the burial by which he was
> buried in a rock,
>
> For the sake of his resurrection
> by which he arose before everyone,
> for the sake of his holy
> household coming from all
> places to Judgement,

I pray, while life lasts, that
you would be our safeguard to
the kingdom of the good Lord,
and that we
go with dear Jesus.[50]

St Thomas Aquinas, at the end of his commentary on the Ave Maria, turns his whole attention to Jesus, the Son of Mary. For it is, in him, Thomas says, in 'the Fruit of the Blessed Virgin', that we find 'sweetness and salvation' and the 'brightness of the Father's glory':

> Therefore let us seek in the Virgin's fruit that which we desire to have. This fruit is blessed by God, because God so filled Him with all grace that it overflows upon us who bow to Him in adoration: 'Blessed be the God and Father of our Lord Jesus Christ, Who has blessed us with every spiritual blessing on high in Christ.' He is blessed by the angels: 'Blessing and glory and wisdom and thanksgiving and honour and power and might be to our God for ever and ever.' And he is blessed by men: 'Let every tongue confess that our Lord Jesus Christ is in the glory of the Father.' 'Blessed is he who

comes in the name of the Lord.' Thus is the Virgin blessed, but still more blessed is her Fruit.[51]

Earlier, in his commentary, St Thomas sets up a contrast between the fruit of Mary's womb, which is the answer to all our desires, and that forbidden fruit, the taste of which Eve had dreamed would give her the knowledge and likeness of a god. But Eve was, of course, deceived: 'For through eating the fruit, Eve did not become like God, but *un*like Him.'[52] In contrast, Mary, the new Eve, 'found in her Fruit [in her Son] all that Eve had desired'.[53] She realised that the life within her womb was divine life, and this fact transformed her utterly. Thomas writes: 'The Blessed Virgin found likeness to God in the Fruit of her womb — and so do all followers of Christ — since through Christ we are united and likened to God.'[54]

What this means — and the idea is remarkable — is that those, in whom Christ is alive, bear like Mary the divine life within them. They contain the uncontainable. St Symeon the New Theologian goes so far as to state that 'just as God, the Word of the Father, entered into the Virgin's womb — even so do we receive the Word in us, as a kind of seed'.[55] And he says further:

> We do not, of course, conceive Him bodily, as did the Virgin and Theotokos, but all the

same we conceive Him in a way which is at once spiritual and substantial. And the One, whom the pure Virgin conceived, we possess in our hearts, as St Paul says: 'God who called the light to shine from the darkness, has shone in our hearts to give us the light of the knowledge of His Son' [2 Cor. 4:6].⁵⁶

The intimate bond between the womb of Mary and the 'tent' of the Church is tellingly underlined in a twelfth-century homily by Blessed Isaac of Stella. Making reference, at one point, to the mystery of the divine indwelling, he makes bold to declare: 'Christ abode for nine months in the tent of Mary's womb; he abides until the consummation of the ages in the tent of the Church's faith. He will abide forever and ever in the knowledge and love of the individual soul.'⁵⁷ Obviously it is not possible for us to penetrate the mystery of Mary's own contemplative experience as the uniquely privileged bearer of the Word. But certain passages in the writings of the saints and mystics can offer us some hint of what Mary's faith-experience might have been. Here, for example, on the theme of the divine indwelling, is a passage of rare spiritual beauty and great depth, taken once again from the writings of St Symeon the New Theologian:

I know that he who is far outside
the whole of creation takes me within himself
and hides me in his arms ...
I, a frail, small mortal in the world,
behold the Creator of the World, all of him,
within myself; and I know
that I shall not die, for I am within Life,
I have the whole of Life springing up
as a fountain within me.
He is in my heart, he is in heaven:
both there and here
he shows himself to me with equal glory.[58]

Part II

A Prayer of the People

Holy Mary,
Mother of God,
pray for us sinners,
now
and at the hour
of our death.

The entire second part of the Hail Mary is different from the first in a number of ways. For a start, it's a more familiar kind of prayer. Like the Our Father it's a prayer of asking, a prayer of petition. But unlike the words in the first part of the Hail Mary, the words here are not taken from Scripture but from Tradition. The prayer, in the form in which we have it today, dates from the end of the fifteenth century. But, before that date, and for a considerable period of time, the faithful had begun adding their own short prayers of intercession to the original Ave Maria. Thus, in or around the year 1440, for example, the Franciscan friar St Bernadine of Siena, after having first repeated in a sermon the two Gospel salutations of the Ave Maria, went on to declare, 'I am unable to prevent myself from adding "Holy Mary, pray for us sinners".'[59]

The version of the prayer as we know it today appeared for the first time in a short treatise composed by the Dominican friar Girolamo Savonarola in 1495.[60] In 1568 this version of the prayer acquired official status when it was included in the reformed Breviary of the Church by the Dominican Pope, St Pius V.[61]

****

A measure of the strength and beauty of the Hail Mary is the devoted attention it has received not only in the world of art and painting over the years, but also within the world of music. The words of the prayer are of such purity and directness, composers of all kinds have been drawn to set the prayer to music. One fairly recent example worth noting is the version by the contemporary Ukranian composer Alexsey Zukharenko. But, of course, in the history of classical music, the two most famous versions are those by

INTRODUCTION

Franz Schubert[62] (1797–1828) and Charles Gounod[63] (1818–93). Many people, I suspect, who do not normally think of themselves as being in any way religious, as soon as they hear performed one or other of these settings of the prayer, may well find that the music touches them to the very depths. Schubert himself, in a letter he wrote to his parents (25 July 1885) regarding his setting of the 'Hymn to the Virgin', noted that many people at the time wondered at the depth and quality of his devotion to Mary: 'They wondered greatly at my piety, which I expressed in a hymn to the Holy Virgin, and which it appears grips every soul and turns it to devotion.'

Chapter 5

'Holy Mary, Mother of God'

The entire second part of the Hail Mary does not include any lines from Scripture. But it is remarkable all the same for the simplicity and depth of its spirituality. *Holy Mary, Mother of God, pray for us sinners, now and at the hour of our death.* Mary is no longer simply addressed as 'Mary'. She is given instead the awesome title 'Mother of God'. For, within her womb, there was contained the infinite fire of God's presence, that fire which, in the burning bush, appeared to Moses and filled him with awe. 'O luminous one,' an early Christian poet exclaims, 'I see a flame, a fire which surrounds you, and I am in awe of it.'[64] Likewise, St Gregory of Nyssa, writing in the fourth century, exclaims:

> O the wonder! The virgin becomes mother and remains virgin ... the virginity does not prevent the childbirth, nor does the child-

> birth destroy the virginity... this seems to me to have been foreshadowed by the theophany of Moses... when the fire kindled the bush and the bush did not wither... so also here.[65]

That the womb of Mary really did contain the fire of the divine presence is something that, for centuries, compelled the wonder of believing Christians. Innumerable, therefore, are the songs, canticles and poems composed in her honour and praise. Writing, for example, in the tenth century, an anonymous Irish poet speaks of her as 'the vessel in which was contained the manna, the shrine which held the King of the stars, the golden cup which contained the wine which gladdens and intoxicates'.[66] Here, as in practically all the Marian canticles, the language instinctively adopted by the poet is the language of ecstasy and love. And that is no bad thing. In fact, for the contemplation of so great and wondrous a mystery there is no language more suitable. Even the sharp and brilliantly controlled syllogisms of the theologian are no match for these graced and humble and passionate texts of devotion.

That said, however, with regard to devotion to Mary, the sober voice of the theologian, the voice of reason and of common sense, is one that very much needs to be heard if the practice of the faith and, in this case, the special honours given to Mary, are to avoid collapsing into mere sentimentality and superstition. 'More numerous than the leaves or blades of grass on a lawn are the tales about Mary.'[67] This is an assertion we find in yet another Irish poem concerning the Mother of God. But – alas – of all the stories to which the poet refers with such enthusiasm, far too many, it has to be said, are simply 'tall tales'! The truth of the matter is that there are few subjects which lend themselves so much to the risk of exaggeration as devotion to the Mother of God.

John Henry Newman, speaking on one occasion of the ways in which our human emotions can be swayed by religion, notes that 'of all passions love is the most unmanageable'.[68] But love, in different degrees and in different forms, is always present in religion. So when it assumes the form of a religious enthusiasm, it too can become unmanageable. Newman writes: 'Religion acts on the affections; who is to hinder these, when once aroused, from gathering in their strength, and running wild?'[69] There is here, of course, a real danger, and it is one Newman will be concerned later to underline. But Newman's first instinct is to defend that natural enthusiasm which accompanies love in all its forms, and which can barely manage to contain itself within the ordinary bonds and limits of custom. He writes:

> I would not give much for that love which is never extravagant, which always observes the proprieties, and can move about in perfect good taste, under all emergencies. What mother, what husband or wife, what youth or maiden in love, but says a thousand foolish things, in the way of endearment, which the speaker would be sorry for strangers to hear; yet they are not on that account unwelcome to the parties to whom they are addressed. Sometimes by bad luck they are written down, sometimes they get into the newspapers; and what might be even graceful, when it was fresh from the heart, and interpreted by the voice and the countenance, presents but a melancholy exhibition when served up cold for the public eye. So it is with devotional feelings.[70]

Newman encourages us here to accept the fact that love, in its own realm, has its own language. We are not, therefore, to be too critical of those exaggerated expressions of love and gratitude to God or to Mary which, on occasion, rise to the lips of devout believers.

Mary can without question be honoured, as anyone else who is loved is honoured, by a hundred beautiful names which ring true in the intimate chamber or in the private chapel of the heart. But what worries Newman is that sometimes intense religious emotion can be translated into confused religious thinking. When that happens, wildly exaggerated notions concerning Mary can begin to take hold in the minds and hearts of believers. And so, against all logic, Mary, the Mother of God, begins to be perceived as more compassionate than her Son, and as possessing even the infinite mercy of God, and as being, therefore, 'the only refuge of those with whom God is angry'.[71] Such notions as these are so utterly and completely mistaken, and so bizarre and wrong-headed, they impress Newman, he tells us openly, 'like a bad dream'.[72] 'I had rather believe', he writes, '... that there is no God at all, than that Mary is greater than God. I will have nothing to do with statements, which can only be explained by being explained away.'[73]

Newman is not for a moment suggesting here that we should not look to Mary, on occasion, to intercede for us with her Son. But the instinctive sense of her care for us, and the deep awareness of the power of her intercession, should never be taken to imply that, between Christ and ourselves, there is somehow an impassable gulf and that Mary is the 'human' bridge between us. That idea is one which would make a complete mockery of the Incarnation. No – Christ, by taking flesh from the womb of Mary, has once and for all crossed the great gulf which had separated the finite and the infinite worlds. He has revealed himself as both God and human – as Son of the Father in heaven and as brother to all humanity on earth: the 'bridge', in other words, that reaches up from ourselves to the Father, and from the Father down to us. He is the world's one, true Mediator: 'For there is only one God, and there is only one mediator between God and mankind, himself a man, Christ Jesus' (I Tim. 2:5).

This great teaching we find repeated throughout the history of the Church, and repeated with particular emphasis in the documents of the Second Vatican Council. We read, for example, in *Lumen Gentium* that with regard precisely to the question of Christ's role as Mediator, 'no [human] creature can ever be counted along with the Incarnate Word and Redeemer.'[74] That does not, of course, deny the fact that all believers are asked by Christ to have some share with him in the work of redemption – to be, as St Paul puts it, 'co-workers with God' (I Cor. 3:9). *Lumen Gentium* states: 'the unique mediation of the Redeemer does not exclude but rather gives rise [among his creatures] to a manifold cooperation which is but a sharing in this one unique source.'[75] There is no mediation, no co-operation of any kind in the work of salvation, except in and through Christ. Even the enormously privileged role given to Mary depends for its very existence on the original grace of her Son's mediation. Her role in no way, therefore, 'obscures or diminishes this unique mediation of Christ, but rather shows its power'.[76] Mary, it is true, at different times and occasions, has been invoked within the Church with titles such as 'advocate' and 'mediatrix'. But 'these titles', the document insists, 'are to be so understood that they neither take away from nor add anything to the dignity and efficacy of Christ the one Mediator'.[77]

****

Given the extraordinary nature and privilege of Mary's role in the plan of salvation, it is no wonder that, at the beginning of the second part of the Hail Mary, her name is linked with the adjective 'holy': '*Holy* Mary, Mother of God, pray for us sinners.' In Mary there is not the least shadow of sin. She is the beloved of God, the one most highly favoured, the virgin found to be with child by the Holy Spirit. In her womb she bore the divine Son. She is the one acknowledged first by the angel, and then by all generations, as 'full of grace'. Her holiness surpasses, therefore, that of all the saints. She is the cause of our joy, the bright morning star, the gate of heaven, the glory of our race.

Hardly, however, have praises of this kind been sung, and I have no doubt that Mary would be the first to remind us that all those who are redeemed by Christ her Son, all who are baptised into his death and resurrection, have already some share in the fullness of grace. Mary is, of course, the first among the redeemed. She is holy, uniquely holy. But all of us who are redeemed, all the people of God, are called to share in the holiness of God, as St Paul makes clear in his letter to the Romans (Rom. 1:7). Such holiness, needless to say, is not something achieved primarily by our own efforts. Like the holiness of Mary itself, it is a holiness dependent entirely on the grace of Christ.

Reflecting on this mystery, St Augustine, in an astonishing passage in his writings, goes so far as to suggest that the individual Christian, when united with Christ, should not be afraid to say 'I am holy!' and to dare to make this declaration in spite of conscious knowledge of the need for continuing purification. Augustine writes:

> The Christian has received the grace of holiness, the grace of baptism and of the

remission of sins ... And since the Apostle [Paul] says of those who have been baptized and cleansed that they are 'sanctified' (*'sanctificatos'*), then let each one of the faithful also say, 'I am holy' (*'Sanctus sum'*). This is not the pride of the man who puffs himself out, but the praise that comes from the one who is not ungrateful. If you claim that you are holy as a result of your own efforts, you are guilty of pride. But if you, who are one of the faithful in Christ, and are a member of Christ, deny that you are holy, you are guilty of ingratitude ... Recognize, then, both that you possess, and that you possess nothing of yourself, so that you may be neither proud nor ungrateful. Say then to God, 'I am holy, because you have sanctified me; because I have received, not because I had anything of my own; because you have given, not because I have deserved.'[78]

****

The supreme title of Mary is Mother of God, a title given to her at the Council of Ephesus in the fifth century. But Mary, the mother of Jesus, is also *our* mother. According to St Albert the Great, '[Mary] conceived us in her heart at the same time as she conceived the divine Word in her womb.'[79] *In her heart.* The Word of God was received and held within Mary's womb. But we were received and held within her heart. I am reminded here of a short poem which was composed many years ago by a woman for her much loved, adopted child. The words of the poem are words which I think Mary would wish to say to each one of us, her adopted children:

> Not flesh of my flesh
> nor bone
> of my bone, but still miraculously
> my own.
>
> Never forget
> for a single minute
> you didn't grow under my heart
> but in it.[80]

Chapter 6

'Pray for us sinners'

———————

One of the truly consoling aspects of Christian faith is the knowledge that, even in times of great failure, when we know we don't deserve help, we can turn to God in prayer and ask for his help, and turn to one another and to the saints. For it is in prayer – perhaps more than anywhere else – that we discover we are not alone. And we make this discovery most of all at the Eucharist. But we are also made aware of the help of grace, and in a particular way, when we turn to Mary: 'Holy Mary, Mother of God, pray for us sinners.'

The Hail Mary is a prayer that can be said in private – a prayer of solitude – or it can be said in public, with others, as when, for example, we recite the Rosary in common. But each time we say the Hail Mary, our prayer is always, in some sense, a prayer said in communion with others. And these 'others' include not only people alive today in the Church and in the world, but also all those, over the centuries, saints and sinners among them, who have repeated these humble words with living faith.

In the opinion of the French Catholic poet, Charles Péguy, 'A sinner can make the best prayer.'[81] He writes: 'No one is more competent than a sinner in matters of Christianity. No one, unless it be a saint.'[82] But then he adds the following, qualifying phrase: 'in principle it is the selfsame man.' A surprising claim, it might appear, but one that is entirely accurate. A saint, after all, is nothing other than a sinner happily converted. And the saints, we know, are outstanding examples for us to follow. But, that said, it is the conviction of Péguy that saints are *not* given to us primarily as ideal exemplars of the Christian Gospel. No – they are men and women with whom we are already, in some sense, in close and intimate contact. Deliberately choosing, on one occasion, to exaggerate this point in order to underline it, he remarked to a friend: 'One is not inspired by the saints, one is in communion with them.'[83] For Péguy what mattered most in our relationship with the saints was that saving 'bond of communion.' He wrote:

> The sinner holds out a hand to the saint, gives a hand to the saint, since the saint gives a hand to the sinner. And all together, one by means of the other, one pulling up

> the other, they ascend to Jesus, they form a chain which ascends to Jesus, a chain of fingers which cannot be unlinked.[84]

As a man and a Christian, Péguy was never afraid to confess his own faults and failings. 'We may have been sinners,' he wrote, 'we were certainly sinners, great sinners ... *pro nobis peccatoribus* ... but we never ceased to be on the right road.'[85] What helped to keep Péguy on that 'road' – his own chosen way of reaching out his hand to touch and hold the hand of Mary – was in simply reciting, over and over again, and with living faith, the Hail Mary. This prayer, he believed, was one which even the most miserable sinner ('le plus lamentable pécheur') could pray with hope. To his friend Lotte, he remarked: 'I am one of those Catholics who would give the whole of St Thomas for the *Stabat*, the *Magnificat*, the *Ave Maria*.'[86] And again: 'In the mechanism of salvation the *Ave Maria* is the last resource. With it one cannot be lost.'[87]

****

When Bernadette Soubirous, the saint of Lourdes, was dying, the last prayer on her lips – not surprisingly – was the Hail Mary. The evening before the actual day she died, Bernadette had asked one of the sisters to help her to 'thank the holy Virgin right up to the end'. Facing death, her main concern was thanksgiving. But then, in the moments just before she died, when the sisters were reciting the Hail Mary close to the chair where she lay, Bernadette, with almost her last breath, was heard to say, and to repeat twice, 'Holy Mary, Mother of God, pray for me, *poor sinner*.'[88]

Since the time of the Second Vatican Council it has been said that people are no longer inclined to turn to Mary for help in the way they did in the past. On one occasion, Cardinal Suenens asked Karl Rahner why he thought this was so, and Rahner replied: 'Christian theologians in our time have made abstractions out of their faith. And abstractions don't need a mother!' Now, for a great number of our contemporaries, including many Christians, the stumbling block in this sentence of Rahner is not the word 'mother', but the word 'need'. People nowadays like to feel they are independent, so the last thing they want to admit to themselves or to others is that they are in need. And yet, in our day-to-day experience, there is nothing more basic or more human. 'Ask and you shall receive,' Jesus advises us in the Gospel, 'seek and you shall find.'

Reflecting on the nature of Christian prayer, St Thomas Aquinas makes a remarkable statement in the *Summa Theologiae*. Because of our utter dependence on God, our Creator and Redeemer, all prayer in the end, Thomas says, and even the prayer of praise and the prayer of thanksgiving, is at root a prayer of petition. All prayer is *asking*. This plain Gospel truth alerts us at once to the value of a simple vocal prayer such as the Hail Mary. But that Gospel truth can be easily obscured. For example, given the fact that some people in the spiritual life are raised to the prayer of quiet and others to the prayer of ecstatic contemplation, a humble vocal prayer like the Hail Mary can begin to appear a very poor cousin indeed. As a result, those of us who never seem to get beyond mere vocal prayer can begin to feel discouraged. But it's worth noting what St Teresa of Avila has to say on the subject. She writes:

> It may seem to anyone who doesn't know about the matter that vocal prayer doesn't go with contemplation; but I know that it does. Pardon me, but I want to say this: I know there are many persons who while praying vocally ... are raised by God to sublime contemplation without their striving for anything or understanding how ... I know a person who was never able to pray any way but vocally, and though she was tied to this form of prayer she experienced everything else. And if she didn't recite vocal prayer her

mind wandered so much that she couldn't bear it. Would that our mental prayer were as good! ... Once she came to me very afflicted because she didn't know how to practice mental prayer nor could she contemplate; she could only pray vocally. I asked her how she was praying, and I saw that though she was tied to the Our Father she experienced pure contemplation and that the Lord was raising her up and joining her with Himself in union. And from her deeds it seemed truly that she was receiving such great favours, for she was living a very good life. So I praised the Lord and envied her for her vocal prayer.[89]

In another place Teresa says: 'No one will ever be able to take from you these books (the Our Father and the Hail Mary), and if you are eager to learn you won't need anything else provided you are humble.'[90] But how do we become humble? Obviously the first thing to do is to admit our failures. But that in itself will never be enough. For if we focus attention only on our sins, we will soon begin to lose all hope. Real humility comes not from keeping our faces in the mud of past failures but in lifting up our eyes from the mud to the throne of mercy. The saints teach us again and again that humility comes more from contemplating the wonderful goodness of God than from contemplating, over and over again, the extent of our own misery. In the medieval text, *The Cloud of Unknowing*, we read:

> I say again to anyone who wants to become a real contemplative like Mary [Magdalene], let the wonderful transcendence and goodness of God teach you humility rather than the thought of your own sinfulness, for then your humility will be perfect. Attend more to the wholly otherness of God than to your own misery.[91]

When we pray, whatever our distress may be, what matters most is that we turn our thoughts with hope to the holiness of God and to the holiness of his saints. And thus, in the Hail Mary, we say: 'Holy Mary, Mother of God, pray for us sinners.' Of all the titles given to Mary by the Church, surely one of the most beautiful is Mother of Mercy. Mary, we know from faith, was conceived and born immaculate. And yet she is the refuge of sinners. Although sinless from the beginning, she is still 'the first among the redeemed'. Now and always, therefore, the very breath she breathes is mercy, and her song is mercy. It might even be said that, since she was preserved free from sin, since she was created immaculate by a unique act of the loving kindness and mercy of God, Mary is closer than any other saint to those most in need of mercy.

****

There is a story concerning Mary's intercession which comes from the very early days of the Dominican Order. At Night Prayer, on one occasion, when the brothers were singing the words of the Salve Regina, 'Turn then, most gracious advocate, your eyes of mercy towards us', one of the brothers saw, in the form of a vision, Mary, the Mother of the Lord, actively interceding in heaven 'for the safety of the whole Order'. The depth of her concern was manifest in one unforgettable detail: while she prayed, Mary was actually seen 'prostrating herself in the presence of her Son'.[92]

Again worth noting in this context is an image which occurs in a poem by the sixteenth-century Irish author Muirchertach Ó Cionga. Writing of the power of Mary's intercession, he declares: 'Mary's wide-extending love is as the growth of a fresh-broken field.'[93] The image is remarkable. It suggests a flourishing which is wholly unexpected and yet somehow natural and very beautiful. And the next line of the poem reads: 'To bring all her race into one home is the marvellous achievement of her breast.'[94] Clearly what Cionga intends to convey here by the word 'race' is all of humanity. But it is not difficult for us to imagine that, with regard to her own 'race' – the people of Israel – Mary's loving intercession extends in a most unique and particular way. William of Newburgh, a monk from Yorkshire in England, writing in the twelfth century, alerts us to this aspect of Mary's active concern. He writes:

> We should know that the merits of the merciful Mother greatly help the salvation of Israel. How insistently do you think, does she daily pray to her omnipotent Son for her race?... Remember, Son, she says, that you have taken your flesh from them, in which and by which you have worked salvation on earth, and that they must share in your spiritual goods, of whose flesh you have not been ashamed. For they ought to have been the first to be saved, because salvation is from them.[95]

****

That Mary, the Mother of Mercy, is someone to whom each one of us, her children, can turn to for help, no matter how apparently hopeless our situation, is something which has been discovered over and over again in every generation. Thus, for example, one of the most celebrated preachers of the eighth century, Paul the Deacon, could announce with manifest ease and confidence that, 'as befits the Mother of Mercy, she is most merciful'. And then, encouraged by the thought of the great kindness of her nature, he could also happily declare: 'she knows how to have compassion on human weakness, because she knows of what we are made.'[96]

Chapter 7

'Now and at the hour of our death'

When, for one reason or another, we contemplate the reality of death, it is not uncommon that we begin to think about the sin and failure in our past. And, for many, this thought can be a cause of great unhappiness and even despair. After all, the past is past, we are told; it can never be recovered; the chance of grace is gone. But when we pray the Hail Mary, there is contained in one small word an entirely different message, and one which can, in itself, completely transform our thinking and transform our lives. It is the word 'now'. 'Pray for us *now*.' What Mary discovered, deep in her being at the Annunciation, was that nothing was impossible to God. In a single moment, in an instant of grace, everything can be changed. And this, of course, is true, or can be true, for each one of us. 'Sometimes', a fourteenth-century Dominican homily declares, 'a man is in a state of damnation before he begins his prayer, and before he is finished he is in a state of salvation.'[97]

St John Climacus, in his book *Stairway to Paradise*, is no less daring in what he says about the potentially powerful effect on our lives of a prayer of one short sentence or even of one small word. Brevity not loquacity is what St John recommends. He writes:

> When you are praying, don't rack your brains to find words. On many occasions the simple monotonous stammering of children has satisfied their Father who is in heaven. Don't bother to be loquacious lest the mind be bewildered in the search for words. The tax-collector gained the Lord's forgiveness with a single sentence, and a single word charged with faith was the salvation of the robber.[98]

One is reminded here of the justly celebrated saying, 'Every saint has a past and every sinner a future.' St Teresa of Avila, reflecting back on her own past life, on one occasion was moved all of a sudden to exclaim: 'Oh, how late have my desires been enkindled …!'[99] Clearly, Teresa was thinking back with regret about how long it took her to turn to God, while God had, for such a long time, been seeking her. In spite of her soul's awareness of such 'time lost', and in spite of the fact, as she admits, that people 'usually say lost time cannot be recovered', Teresa, remembering Christ and his great power and mercy, makes bold to declare, 'You, Lord, can win this time back again.'[100] And she prays: 'O Lord, I confess Your great power. If You are powerful, as You are, what is impossible for You who can do everything?' And again: 'although I am miserable, I firmly believe You can do what You desire.'[101] Full of confidence in the quiet, transforming grace of *now*, Teresa's prayer concludes: 'Recover, my God, the lost time by giving me grace in the present ... for if You want to You can do so.'[102]

In our lives, we can say that there are only two moments that are of supreme importance: the moment of our death, and this moment now, the present moment. Part of the greatness of the Hail Mary is that it contains, and contains together in one breath, as it were, both of these moments:

Mother of God, pray for us now and at the hour of our death.

Of the many beautiful prayers addressed to Mary my favourite by far is the Hail Mary. However, by way of conclusion now, I'd like to draw attention to another prayer or meditation addressed to Mary. It's a prayer composed in manifest poverty of spirit, but also in profound hope, by the eleventh-century monk St Anselm.

> Mother of the life of my soul,
> nurse of the Redeemer of my flesh,
> who gave suck to the Saviour
> of my whole being ...
> Mary, I beg you, by that grace
> through which the Lord is with you,
> and you willed to be with him,
> let your mercy be with me,
> let love for you always be with me,
> and the care of me be always
> with you.[103]

Notes

1 This reflection took the form of a sermon or series of sermons delivered perhaps in Paris or in Naples. The uncertainty regarding time and place is discussed by Jean-Pierre Torrell in *St Thomas Aquinas: The Person and His Work*, trans. R. Royal (Washington: Catholic University of America Press, 1996), pp. 71–2 and 358. One man (John of Blasio) claimed to have been present in the church at Naples when the reflection was delivered. He says of St Thomas that 'he preached with his eyes shut and his mind in heaven'. See 'The First Canonization Enquiry', in *The Life of Saint Thomas Aquinas: Biographical Documents*, trans. Kenelm Foster OP (London: Longmans, 1959), p. 105. The quality of St Thomas's personal devotion to the Virgin is indicated by one tiny but eloquent detail. In the incomplete autograph of the *Summa contra Gentiles* (which exists today in the Vatican Library) on a number of occasions, in the margins of the text, St Thomas writes 'Ave'.

2 See 'Address of Hans Urs von Balthasar', in *L'Osservatore Romano* (English edn), 23 July 1984, p. 8. This address was given by von Balthasar on 25 June 1984, after he had

received the 'International Paul VI Prize' in the presence of Pope John Paul II.

3 See J. de Guibert, 'Ave Maria', in *Dictionnaire de Spiritualité*, vol. I (Paris: Cerf, 1987), p. 1164.

4 One obvious difference between the Lucan passage and the text of the prayer is that, in Luke 1:28, the name Mary is not actually mentioned by the angel.

5 St Thomas Aquinas, *The Three Greatest Prayers: Commentaries on the Lord's Prayer, the Hail Mary, and the Apostle's Creed* (Manchester NH: Sophia Institute Press, 1990), p. 164.

6 Aquinas, *The Three Greatest Prayers*, p. 165. The term 'full of grace' derives from the Latin phrase *gratia plena*, a phrase St Jerome uses in his Vulgate translation. In the original Greek of St Luke, however, the term used was *kecharitōmenē*, a word that, in the Jerusalem Bible, is translated more accurately as 'so highly favoured'.

7 'The Akathistos Hymn' (author unknown), *The Penguin Book of Greek Verse*, ed. C. A. Trypanis (London: Penguin, 1971), pp. 374–5. What particularly distinguishes this hymn of the Greek Church is the easeful way it unites doctrinal statement, popular piety and the grace of a liturgical form.

8 Julian of Norwich, *Revelations of Divine Love* (the longer text), trans. C. Wolters (London: Burns and Oates, 1966), p. 71.

9 Julian of Norwich, *Showings* (the shorter text), trans. E. Colledge and J. Walsh (New York: Paulist Press, 1978), p. 131.

10 See René Laurentin, *Bernadette Speaks: A Life of Saint Bernadette Soubirous in Her Own Words*, trans. J. W. Lynch and R. DesRosiers (Boston: Pauline Books and Media, 2000), pp. 20 and 42.

11 Laurentin, *Bernadette Speaks*, pp. 218 and 508.

12 St Bernadette, although she came under enormous pressure to deny the fact, kept insisting all through her life that the radiant figure she saw at Massabielle was a girl no bigger than herself. See René Laurentin, *Lourdes: Histoire authentiques des apparitions*, vol. I (Paris: Lethielleux, 1961), p. 153.

13 This astonishing statement refers, of course, not to the mystery of Mary's virginal motherhood but to the fact that, from the moment of her conception, Mary – chosen to be the mother of the Son of God – was preserved free from the taint of all sin.

14 See 'Le Carnet jaune', in *Thérèse de Lisieux: Oeuvres complètes* (Paris: Cerf, 2001), p. 1103.

15 'Le Carnet jaune', p. 1103.

16 St Thomas Aquinas, '*Responsio ad Lectorem Bisuntinum*', no. 939, in *Opuscula Theologica*, vol. I (Rome: Marietti, 1954), p. 244.

17 'Le Carnet jaune', p. 1103.

18 Paul VI, *Marialis Cultus: Apostolic Exhortation for the Right Ordering and Development of Devotion to the Blessed Mary*, 57 (Rome: Vatican Polyglot Press, 1974), pp. 88–9.

19 Ildephonsus of Toledo, *De virginitate perpetua sanctae Mariae*, 12, Migne, *PL* 96, 105C; cited in Luigi Gambero, *Mary in the Middle Ages: The Blessed Virgin in the Thought of Medieval Latin Theologians*, trans. T. Buffer (San Francisco: Ignatius Press, 2000), p. 34.

20 Ildephonsus of Toledo, *De virginitate perpetua sanctae Mariae*, 12, Migne, *PL* 96, 105C; cited in Gambero, *Mary in the Middle Ages*, p. 34.

21 The sermon *In Annuntiationem*, from which this extract is taken, was delivered by St Gregory of Nyssa some time

between 370 and 380. For a modern edition of the text, see Davide M. Montagna, 'La Lode alla Theotokos nei secoli IV–VII', *Marianum*, 24, IV (1962), pp. 503–4.

22 Denise Levertov, 'Annunciation', in *A Door in the Hive* (New York: New Directions, 1989), p. 86.

23 Levertov, 'Annunciation', p. 88.

24 Levertov, 'Annunciation', p. 87.

25 Levertov, 'Annunciation', p. 87.

26 St Bernard's homily 'In Praise of the Virgin Mary' is included in the Office of Readings for 20 December in the Roman Breviary, vol. I (London: Collins, 1974), pp. 141–2.

27 Levertov, 'Annunciation', pp. 86–7.

28 Levertov, 'Annunciation', p. 87.

29 Levertov, 'Annunciation', p. 87.

30 Levertov, 'Annunciation', pp. 87–8.

31 St Teresa of Avila, 'Meditations on the Song of Songs', *The Collected Works of St Teresa of Avila*, vol. 2, trans. K. Kavanaugh and O. Rodriquez (Washington DC: Institute of Carmelite Studies, 1980), p. 253.

32 Meister Eckhart, 'Counsels on Discernment', in *Meister Eckhart: Essential Sermons, Commentaries, Treatises, and Defense*, trans. E. Colledge and B. McGinn (London: SPCK, 1981), p. 260.

33 John Henry Newman, 'The Theory of Developments in Religious Doctrine', Sermon XV, in *Oxford University Sermons* (Westminster MD, Christian Classics, 1966; originally published 1843), p. 313.

34 Newman, 'The Theory of Developments', pp. 313–14. In a memorable phrase from a homily of the fourth century, Mary is described as 'the table at which faith sits in thought'. See Pseudo-Epiphanius, *Homily in Praise of the Holy Mother of*

God, Migne, *PG* 43, 493; cited in John Paul II, *Fides et Ratio: On the Relationship between Faith and Reason* (Boston: Pauline Books, 1998), p. 130.

35 Ildephonsus of Toledo, *Liber de virginitate perpetua sanctae Mariae*, I, Migne, *PL* 96, 58C; cited in Gambero, *Mary in the Middle Ages*, pp. 32–3.

36 St Jerome, in his Vulgate translation of St Luke's gospel, translated the Greek word *Chaire* with the Latin word *Ave* ('Hail'). Jerome came to this decision because *Chaire* ('Rejoice') was, at that time, the ordinary way of greeting in the Greek world. But the word 'Rejoice', in St Luke's text, expresses something much greater than the warmth of a simple greeting. It was intended as a conscious evocation – an echo and a fulfilment – of the great announcement of salvation by the Old Testament prophets. Here one thinks immediately of lines such as the following from *Zechariah*: 'Rejoice heart and soul, daughter of Zion! Shout with gladness, daughter of Jerusalem! See now, your king comes to you; he is victorious, he is triumphant, humble and riding on a donkey' (Zech. 9:9).

37 St Teresa of Avila, 'Spiritual Testimonies', in *Collected Works*, vol. 1, trans. Kavanaugh and Rodriguez, p. 390.

38 St Teresa of Avila, 'Spiritual Testimonies', pp. 390–9. Are we to conclude, then, that Jesus really did appear to his mother after the resurrection? With regard to this question, all four gospels and the Acts of the Apostles are silent. And, for many believers, that fact is a sufficiently clear indication that the event simply never took place. But, in the New Testament itself, towards the end of St John's gospel, we are reminded that there were 'many things Jesus did' which were not

written down. So the truth of the matter is by no means clear. What is interesting to note is that, already by the fourth century, the idea had found general acceptance among the Fathers of the Church. Pope John Paul II, in a reflection he delivered on Easter Monday, 4 April 1994, remarked: 'The Scriptures do not mention this but it is a conviction based on the fact that Mary was Christ's mother, his faithful mother, his dearest mother.' See *L'Osservatore Romano*, English edn (13 April 1994), p. 3. See also C. Gianelli, 'Témoignages patristiques en faveur d'une apparition du Christ ressuscité á Vierge Marie', *Revue d'Études Byzantines* XI (1953), *Mélanges Martin Jugie*, pp. 106–9; J. D. Breckenridge, 'Et prima vidit: The Iconography of the Appearance of Christ to his Mother', *Art Bulletin* 39 (1957), pp. 9–32.

39 Bláthmac Mac Con Brettan, 'A Poem to Mary', in *The New Oxford Book of Irish Verse*, ed. and trans. Thomas Kinsella (Oxford: Oxford University Press, 1986), p. 15.

40 Entitled *Monita salutaria B.V. Mariae ad cultures suos indiscretos*, Adam Widenfeld's text originally appeared in the winter of 1673. See 'Les Avis Salutaires', in *Theotokos: A Theological Encyclopedia of the Blessed Virgin Mary*, ed. Michael O'Carroll (Dublin: Dominican Publications, 1982), pp. 66–7. See also Paul Hoffer, *La dévotion à Marie au déclin du XVIIe siècle* (Paris: Cerf, 1938).

41 St John Chrysostom, *Homily on St Matthew's Gospel*, 50, *PG* 58, 508–9.

42 St Gregory of Nyssa, extract from a sermon *In Annuntiationem Deiparae*, which, for centuries, had been mistakenly attributed to St John Chrysostom. See Migne, *PG* 62, 765.

43 Jacob of Serugh, 'Homily I: On the Mother of God', in *S. Martryii, qui et Sahdona quae supersunt omnia*, ed. Paul Bedjanpage (Paris, 1902), pp. 638–9. See also *Jacob of Serug: On the Mother of God*, trans. M. Hansbury (Crestwood NY: St Vladimir's Seminary Press, 1998), p. 41. St Thérèse of Lisieux, in one of the plays she composed for her Carmelite community, places the following sentence on the lips of Mary, the young mother of Jesus: 'I am astonished that a little milk is necessary for the existence of the One who gives life to the world.' See 'La Fuite en Égypte', in *Sainte Thérèse de Lisieux: Oeuvres complètes*, p. 888.

44 See 'Le Carnet jaune', p. 1103.

45 Julian of Norwich, *Revelations of Divine Love* (the longer text), p. 101.

46 St Anselm, 'Prayer to St Mary'. See *In Praise of Mary*, ed. Donal Flanagan (Dublin: Veritas Publications, 1975), p. 111.

47 John Paul II, *Rosarium Virginis Mariae: Apostolic Letter on the Most Holy Rosary*, p. 42, n. 33.

48 John Paul II, *Rosarium Virginis Mariae*, p. 42, n. 33.

49 John Paul II, *Rosarium Virginis Mariae*, p. 36, n. 26.

50 St Columcille, 'Invocation of the Blessed Virgin Mary', in *Early Irish Lyrics: Eighth to Twelfth Century*, ed. Gerard Murphy (Oxford: Clarendon Press, 1956), pp. 49–51.

51 Aquinas, *The Three Greatest Prayers*, p. 172.

52 Aquinas, *The Three Greatest Prayers*, p. 171.

53 Aquinas, *The Three Greatest Prayers*, p. 171.

54 Aquinas, *The Three Greatest Prayers*, p. 171.

55 St Symeon the New Theologian (949–1022), *On the Mystical Life: The Ethical Discourses*, vol. I, *The Church and the Last Things*,

trans. A. Golitzin (Crestwood NY: St Vladimir's Seminary Press, 1995), p. 55.
56 St Symeon, *On the Mystical Life*, pp. 55–6.
57 Isaac of Stella (1100–c. 1169), *Sermo in Assumptione Beatae Mariae*, LI, Migne, *PL* 194, 1865C.
58 A text from St Symeon the New Theologian; cited in *The Orthodox Way*, ed. Kallistos Ware (Oxford: Mowbray, 1979), p. 32.
59 Cited in de Guibert, 'Ave Maria', p. 1164. For further information on the history of the Hail Mary, see René Laurentin, *Je vous salue Marie* (Paris: Desclée, 1989) and Servais Pinckaers, *La Grâce de Marie* (Paris: Médiaspaul, 1989).
60 Savonarola's treatise was entitled *L'Exposizione sopra l'Ave Maria*. The prayer is printed in Latin on the first page of the treatise. It reads: *Ave Maria gratia plena Dominus tecum Benedicta tu in mulieribus et benedictus fructus ventri tui Jesus Sancta Maria mater Dei ora pro nobis peccatoribus nunc et in hora mortis. Amen.* See de Guibert, 'Ave Maria', p. 1164. Only one small word is missing from the Savonarola version, the word *nostrae* (our).
61 De Guibert, 'Ave Maria', p. 1164.
62 The actual words of the Ave Maria are not the words Schubert originally set to music. The text he used (a work by Sir Walter Scott in German translation) did, however, include lines of a hymn-like quality which were addressed to Mary and recalled something of the spirit of the Ave Maria prayer. The person responsible for setting the Latin Ave Maria to the music of Schubert remains unknown to this day. Other composers of settings for the prayer include Giovanni Pierluigi da Palestrina (1526–94), Orlando di

Lasso (1532–94), Giuseppe Verdi (1813–1901) and Igor Stravinskij (1882–1971).

63 The Gounod setting adds melody and words to a prelude which formed part of a collection of preludes and fugues, originally composed by Johann Sebastian Bach and entitled 'The Well-Tempered Clavier'.

64 St Romanos the Melodious (*c.* 490–*c.* 556), 'On the Annunciation', I. See *Romano il Melode: Inni*, ed. G. Gharib (Rome: Paoline, 1981), p. 15.

65 St Gregory Nyssa, '*Oratio in diem natalem Christi*', PG 46, 1136A, B.

66 This Irish poem takes the form of a night-prayer of intercession. Mary is asked by the poet to bring him safely and swiftly to heaven, 'to lead him by the hand'. See Peter O'Dwyer, 'Mary in the Irish Tradition', in *Mary in the Church*, ed. J. Hyland (Athlone: Veritas, 1989), pp. 149–50, 185.

67 A line from a poem by the sixteenth-century Irish poet Aongus Fionn Ó Dálaigh; cited in O'Dwyer, 'Mary in the Irish Tradition', p. 155.

68 John Henry Newman, *Certain Difficulties Felt by Anglicans*, vol. 2, new edition (London, 1892) p. 80.

69 Newman, *Certain Difficulties*, p. 79.

70 Newman, *Certain Difficulties*, p. 80.

71 Newman, *Certain Difficulties*, p. 113.

72 Newman, *Certain Difficulties*, p. 114.

73 Newman, *Certain* Difficulties, p. 115.

74 *Lumen Gentium: Dogmatic Constitution on the Church*, 62, in *Vatican Council II: The Conciliar and Post Conciliar Documents*, trans. A. Flannery (Dublin: Dominican Publications, 1996), p. 419.

75 *Lumen Gentium*, 62, p. 419..

76 *Lumen Gentium*, 60, p. 418.

77 *Lumen Gentium*, 62, p. 419.

78 St Augustine, *Enarratio in Psalmum* 85, 4, *PL* 37, 1084.

79 St Albert the Great, *In Evangelium secundum Lucam* (Luke 10:42), *Opera omnia*, vol. 23, ed. E. Borgnet (Paris, 1895), p. 90.

80 This simple but striking poem is most often attributed to the writer Fleur Heylinger.

81 Charles Péguy, 'Sinners and Saints', in *Basic Verities, Charles Péguy: Poetry and Prose*, trans. Ann and Julian Greene (New York: Pantheon Books, 1943), p. 179.

82 Charles Péguy, 'The Christian Life', in *Basic Verities*, p. 181.

83 Péguy to M. Laudet; cited in Marjorie Villiers, *Charles Péguy: A Study in Integrity* (London: Collins, 1965), p. 277. Pope St Leo the Great strikes a similar note when speaking on one occasion about the holiness of Christ. In order to shock us into an awareness of the point he wants to make, he writes: 'Christus non est exemplum sed mysterium', literally translated, 'Christ is not our example but mystery.' I take this to mean: Yes, Christ *is* indeed our example, but he is so much more. He is God present to us, with us and in us.

84 Péguy, 'The Christian Life', pp. 181–3. 'Mary, take this hand in yours!' marks the beginning of a poem by the sixteenth-century Irish poet Aongus Fionn Ó Dálaigh. See O'Dwyer, 'Mary in the Irish Tradition', p. 155.

85 Péguy to M. le Grix; cited in Villiers (ed.), *Charles Péguy*, p. 277.

86 Péguy to Lotte, conversation: 3 April 1912, *Lettres et entretiens* (Paris, 1927), pp. 151–2.

87 Péguy to Lotte, *Lettres et entretiens*, pp. 171–2.

88 See René Laurentin, *Bernadette of Lourdes: A Life Based on Authenticated Documents*, trans. J. Drury (London: Darton, Longman & Todd, 1979), p. 239.

89 St Teresa of Avila, 'The Way of Perfection', ch. 30, in *Collected Works*, vol. 2, trans. Kavanaugh and Rodriquez, p. 152.

90 St Teresa of Avila, 'The Way of Perfection', ch. 21, in *Collected Works*, vol. 2, trans. Kavanaugh and Rodriquez, p. 118.

91 *The Cloud of Unknowing*, ch. 23, trans. William Johnston (New York: Image Books, 1973), p. 79.

92 See Jordan of Saxony, '[*Libellus*]: *On the Beginnings of the Order of Preachers*, trans. S. Tugwell (Dublin: Dominican Publications, 1982), p. 31.

93 Lines from a poem by Muirchertach Ó Cionga; cited by O'Dwyer in 'Mary in the Irish Tradition', p. 155.

94 Ó Cionga, cited by O'Dwyer in 'Mary in the Irish Tradition', p. 155.

95 William of Newburgh (1136?–1198?), *On the Song of Songs*, 3.5, 152; cited in Hilda Graef, *Mary: A History of Doctrine and Devotion* (London: Sheed & Ward, 1985), p. 259.

96 Paul the Deacon, *In Assumptione beatae Mariae*, I, *PL* 95, 1496B; cited in Gambero, *Mary in the Middle Ages*, p. 57.

97 William Peraldus, 'Homily on Prayer', in *Early Dominicans*, ed. Simon Tugwell, The Classics of Western Spirituality (New York: Paulist Press, 1982), p. 168.

98 St John Climacus, *Stairway to Paradise*, 28, *PG* 88, 1132; cited in *Drinking from a Hidden Fountain: A Patristic Breviary*, ed. Thomas Spidlik (London: New City, 1992), p. 366.

99 St Teresa of Avila, 'Soliloquies', in *Collected Works*, vol. 1, trans. Kavanaugh and Rodriquez, p. 446.

100 St Teresa of Avila, 'Soliloquies', p. 447.

NOTES

101 St Teresa of Avila, 'Soliloquies', p. 447.
102 St Teresa of Avila, 'Soliloquies', p. 447.
103 Lines from St Anselm's 'Prayer to St Mary'. See Flanaghan (ed.), *In Praise of Mary*, p. 110.